PRAISE FOR
THE OTHER SOFT SKILL

I speak to business owners and corporate executives daily about how to train their leaders and managers to communicate effectively to their workforce, often emphasizing how dramatic an effect it can have on their bottom line. In today's workplace, recognizing, knowing, and understanding generational differences and how they affect your team is an essential skill for all leaders. If you want to unlock the hidden power of your team, start with Dr. Carrie Root's book. *The Other Soft Skill* is a blueprint for success based on unlocking the power of generational intelligence and shared experience. I highly recommend it.

—**Mark Koulianos,** *Executive Director, USF Office of Corporate Training and Professional Education*

The Other Soft Skill is a valuable read for everyone in today's workforce to identify and guide our motivators and worldviews. Dr. Root shares information that can easily be used as a team-building tool to not only explore, but also to provide a solid impact on how our own worldviews shape our interactions with others.

—**Trenton Hightower,** *CEO, GradCast; Author.* Field Trip 101

T0163805

I wish I had this book forty years ago! Dr. Carrie Root brings to light the missing voice to understand what we have lost when communicating across generational divides. It is essential to discover how "the other soft skill" elevates your workforce, improves working across the aisle, and strengthens your organization to flourish, making this book your hidden armament of long-term professional success.

—**Ken Dambrosio,** *Former President, Cote and D'Ambrosio; 2006 Gold Stevie Award Recipient*

The Other Soft Skill is an enlightening window into the world of generational intelligence. Dr. Carrie Root has used her years of extensive experience working in a multitude of industries to accentuate the importance of understanding generational intelligence and communication. This book gives specific details on how to succeed in multigenerational environments and is a must-have handbook for current and future leaders of *any* generation! From the classroom to the boardroom, these techniques have already changed how I approach generational differences.

—**James P. Getman, PhD, MBA,** *Program Director, University of Saint Katherine*

As a member of the baby boomer generation who continues to have the privilege to lead, serve, and to develop winning teams of people from multiple generations with diverse backgrounds, Dr. Carrie Root's book is absolutely superb!

She has brilliantly captured the need for us to understand and leverage generational intelligence as one of the most important soft skills during this unique period in history wherein there are sometimes five generations of people within the workforce.

This book is essential reading for all who serve as leaders and for all who seek to understand the art and science of effective leadership and followership within a diverse workforce and society.

—Vice Admiral Mel Williams Jr., US Navy (retired), *Coauthor,* Navigating the Seven Seas

Dr. Carrie Root sheds light on a lesser known soft skill that has a big impact on teams—generational intelligence. Especially in a post-COVID-19 world where so many of us are working remotely, every leader who wants to improve productivity and communication must read this pioneering book in order to gain a deeper understanding of their teams, which likely represent a handful, if not all five, of the existing generations working together today.

—**Aránzazu Ascunce, PhD,** *Educational Developer and Coach, Catholic University of America*

THE OTHER
Soft Skill

Carrie Root, PhD

THE OTHER
Soft Skill

How to Solve Workplace Challenges
with Generational Intelligence

Published by Advantage, Charleston, South Carolina.
Member of Advantage Media Group.

ADVANTAGE is a registered trademark, and the Advantage colophon is a trademark of Advantage Media Group, Inc.

Printed in the United States of America.

10 9 8 7 6 5 4 3 2 1

ISBN: 978-1-64225-298-9
LCCN: 2021915256

Book design by Mary Hamilton.

This publication is designed to provide accurate and authoritative information in regard to the subject matter covered. It is sold with the understanding that the publisher is not engaged in rendering legal, accounting, or other professional services. If legal advice or other expert assistance is required, the services of a competent professional person should be sought.

Advantage Media Group is proud to be a part of the Tree Neutral® program. Tree Neutral offsets the number of trees consumed in the production and printing of this book by taking proactive steps such as planting trees in direct proportion to the number of trees used to print books. To learn more about Tree Neutral, please visit **www.treeneutral.com**.

Advantage Media Group is a publisher of business, self-improvement, and professional development books and online learning. We help entrepreneurs, business leaders, and professionals share their Stories, Passion, and Knowledge to help others Learn & Grow. Do you have a manuscript or book idea that you would like us to consider for publishing? Please visit **advantagefamily.com** or call **1.866.775.1696**.

To my muses, Dana and Mary

CONTENTS

INTRODUCTION 1
Generational Intelligence

CHAPTER ONE 11
Confronting Communication
Challenges through
Generational Intelligence

CHAPTER TWO 25
Understanding Generational
Motivators

CHAPTER THREE 37
Understanding How Teams Work

CHAPTER FOUR 49
Overcoming Biases

CONCLUSION 63

ACKNOWLEDGMENTS 67

ABOUT THE AUTHOR 71

GET IN TOUCH 73

OUR MOTIVATING
MUSIC PLAYLIST 75

Generational Intelligence

The Other Soft Skill

In developing a course that trains professionals for today's challenging multigenerational workplace, my colleagues and I decided that it would be memorable (and fun) to incorporate interactive exercises. During one such exercise, we place images of phones representing different eras—rotary dial phones, princess phones with touch tone, early cordless phones, flip phones, and iPhones—around the room, asking participants to stand beside the one that best represents the phone they grew up using.

Traditionalists choose the rotary dial phones, and their conversations revolve around growing up without privacy or answering machines. Explaining what party lines were often comes as a surprise to younger attendees. Princess phone users recall memories of stretching the phone and handset cords to the limit to reach a private place for a conversation. The cordless phones draw people who remember having conversations wherever they wanted with the handset, and later searching for the handset and finding it uncharged after being off the base. And then, of course, there is the smartphone generation, who have grown up with near-instant access for family and friends with the world's knowledge available on their phone.

When I first took this workshop, I chose the rotary dial phone. In my group was a young woman, twenty-five years younger than me. My bias from her appearance was that she and I could not have the same phone in common from our youth.

How wrong I was! I learned from her that she grew up in Rwanda, a country whose technology wasn't as advanced as that of the US. I initially saw her as a different generation, and until we had a conversation about her worldview, I had a different set of expectations for her and didn't realize how similar some of our early experiences were.

Socioeconomic conditions impact which technology is present in a young person's life. A Gen Xer was in my group who grew up in very limited financial conditions, and their family was happy that their house had a phone, even if it was a rotary-dial heavy clunker.

That's why it's important to explore the worldview of the individuals you interact with, or you'll wind up like I did, with a set of wrong assumptions about them. It takes less energy to get to know a person than the energy required to untangle the damage working with a bad set of assumptions can do to a relationship. It takes generational intelligence and a willingness to set aside your biases and explore another person's worldview.

Generational Intelligence: The Other Soft Skill

Soft skills are at the top of an employer's list of desired skills because they have a direct impact on the performance of an employee. Think of soft skills as nontechnical skills that affect how you interact and solve problems at work. As Rick Stephens, senior vice president of human resources at Boeing Corporation, said,

Soft skills are at the top of an employer's list of desired skills because they have a direct impact on the performance of an employee.

"We hire for hard skills. We fire for soft skills. The ability to interact and communicate with others or behave ethically and take responsibility for things tends to be where people normally break down."[1]

There are four soft skills that are widely accepted as the most important soft skills to embrace in the workplace: emotional intelligence, communication skills, critical thinking and problem solving, and adaptability. Add to these basic employer expectations: showing up on time to work, focusing your energies on your job and not your phone, and answering emails.

These topics get a lot of attention. But the issues that come up regarding generational intelligence are more subtle, and they require a different conversation. And they are not exclusive to the new employee. Cross-generational issues arise up and down the ranks of leadership.

It's also a soft skill to recognize where we are different and where we are the same. It's a soft skill to recognize your biases. Each generation has its own separate set of experiences. We call these "worldviews." Because of differing worldviews, each generation tends

---

1   Priyanka Madhusudan, "How to Balance Hard Skills and Soft Skills Training," People Matters, January 13, 2018, accessed April 2021, https://www.peoplematters.in/article/skilling/how-to-balance-hard-skills-and-soft-skills-training-17239.

to have varying expectations of age-different others. It is akin to diversity awareness—we are all different. But if we explore our worldviews together, we will find we share common experiences.

As of this writing, there are five generations in the workforce. From oldest to youngest, these are known as the Traditionalist, Baby Boomer, Gen X, Millennial, and Gen Z generations. These generations are defined by world events, personal experiences, and technology.

While our workplaces were rocked by the Millennial generation over the past two decades, 28 percent of management positions are now held by Millennials, and they are strongly changing organizational cultures.[2] And even though Millennials had to bear the older generations stereotyping them as having a poor work ethic, they in turn have concerns about how Gen Zs are going to impact the culture of the workplace.[3]

---

2   Kerri Anne Renzulli, "28% of Millennials Are Managers Now—Here Are 5 Ways They're Changing the Office," CNBC Make It, March 6, 2019, accessed April 2021, https://www.cnbc.com/2019/03/05/5-ways-millennial-managers-are-changing-the-office.html.

3   Ruth Umoh, "Here's How Millennials Feel About the Next Generation Entering the Workforce," CNBC Make It, November 7, 2017, accessed April 2021, https://www.cnbc.com/2017/11/07/why-millennials-arent-happy-that-gen-z-is-entering-the-workforce.html.

It is time that organizations address generational differences through professional development training. It is time we got savvy instead of pointing fingers as was done with the Millennial generation and now appears to be happening with the emerging Gen Z generation. There are many soft skills that are critical to a productively running organization, but there is another soft skill that needs to gain a foothold alongside leadership skills, interpersonal skills, and communication skills. This book explores that other soft skill: generational intelligence.

Developing your generational intelligence means employing skills like understanding those events that brought about the different generational characteristics, recognizing your own biases, and practicing active listening to understand someone else's worldview. This will give you insight on how better to communicate and collaborate with age-other individuals. It will also provide insights on how to motivate and reward age-other individuals.

In a multigenerational workforce, there are challenges—in communication, teamwork, motivation, and recognizing biases. But when generational intelligence is employed, these challenges can be recognized and resolved, which improves the workplace environment for the benefit of the organization. When workers are happy, they stick around and do great work, making the organization thrive. That's the goal.

> **When workers are happy, they stick around and do great work, making the organization thrive.**

How I Got Here

A number of things came together around the same time. In my work as a high-level troubleshooter, I began to see issues with how teams worked together. It took me quite a while to recognize what I was seeing, but upon reflection I began to realize that I was actually looking at breakdowns in how people communicate. I saw a mismatch in their expectations of each other.

This was also around the time I had joined the nonprofit service organization Rotary International and became interested through my club in a statewide scholarship program that offered four-year scholarships to at-risk youth as a motivator to complete high school. This successful program has increased graduation rates from 36 percent to over 90 percent in the almost four decades it has been in existence. But I wanted to know what happened to those students after high school. Did they get degrees? Did they get appropriate employment? I found that only 40 percent earned any type of credential through this program. When speaking with large local employers, I learned that they had very low expectations about hiring from the community colleges. They would find diamonds in the rough, but they were too rough.

A few years ago, Google released a report after studying the impact of their hiring strategies on the success of their organization. Traditionally, Google hired the best and brightest STEM candidates. But when they looked at their HR data regarding what characteristics were associated with their strongest performers, STEM ranked *last*! The important skills their top performers had were strong soft skills.[4]

In skills gap studies across the US, companies were reporting, "Look, we can train the hard skills; send us people who know how to show up on time, are able to work with teams, and can think critically."

From all this, I saw a challenge and an opportunity. I'm like a pit bull with a pork chop when I see a challenge. That led me to form my company, Alpha UMi, to support my quest to make excep-

---

4   Valerie Strauss, "The Surprising Thing Google Learned About Its Employees—and What It Means for Today's Students," *The Washington Post*, December 20, 2017, https://www.washington-post.com/news/answer-sheet/wp/2017/12/20/the-surprising-thing-google-learned-about-its-employees-and-what-it-means-for-todays-students/.

tional professional development training products available that promote the growth of great soft skills, particularly generational intelligence, for the benefit of our workforce.

In This Book

I'm glad you're taking this first step in learning how generational intelligence is crucial in today's workforce. In this book, we'll explore soft skills that are often overlooked. We'll look at the challenges facing our multigenerational workplace leadership and examine how the other soft skill, generational intelligence, is a critical skill for effectively working with "age-other" individuals.

The divide caused by generational differences is not unique to now and likely won't end anytime soon. That's why multigenerational challenges in communication, motivations, teamwork, preset expectations, and biases must be explored and understood now through the lens of generational intelligence.

CHAPTER ONE

Confronting Communication Challenges through Generational Intelligence

Most people want a connection. We all want to find common ground with one another. Think of the story of the gurgle pot, a delightful pitcher that makes gurgling noises as you pour water from it. The designer of my gurgle pot, Matt Ellison, shares his inspiration:[5]

---

5   Matt Ellison, "About," GurglePot.com, accessed April 2021, http://www.gurglepot.com/about.html.

Years ago, I attended my brother's wedding in a small village in Southern France. Since there were no hotels in town, all guests were matched with French hosts. My hosts spoke no English, and I spoke no French, which made dinner conversation a challenge. Long stretches of awkward silences were compounded by the fact that French dinners can last three to four hours. There was, however, one saving grace … a fish-shaped water pitcher that "gurgled." I found myself drinking more water than wine so I could fill the silent room with "gurgling" and unite the table with smiles.

What made for an opportunity with the gurgle pot was the obviousness of the communication barrier caused by language. When the communication barrier is caused by technology, age differences, or bias, it's not as easy to see or understand.

In this chapter we'll discuss what generational communication challenges look like, how this impacts productivity and building relationships, and how generational intelligence can help you work through these challenges and, ultimately, make meaningful connections.

Recognizing Generational Communication Challenges

A communication challenge confronted most often in the workplace happens when individuals have their own preferred ways to receive information. These preferences often trend with each generation.

Consider the case of a young Realtor working with a senior couple downsizing from home to condo. The older couple will likely want more face-to-face support, from being taken around to see properties to having contracts explained. They may want phone calls to set up appointments. They may not have the ability or trust to sign documents electronically. Contrast this to the young Realtor's younger clients who want digital links to properties, will communicate almost exclusively via text, drive by properties on their own, and execute contracts electronically. That young Realtor needs to recognize the different work styles required by these two different generations of clients.

Similar logic can be applied to other businesses. Consider insurance companies. Older generations prefer a voice. Think of doctors' offices that are trying to go digital with patient portals. These are embraced by younger generations, but the older generations still want to talk to someone. If an individual's communication needs are not being met, they will likely seek another provider who can communicate with them in a way they feel comfortable.

Learn to recognize specific preferences in generations other than our own, so we can adjust our expectations accordingly.

Learn to recognize specific preferences in generations other than our own, so we can adjust our expectations accordingly.

For example, older generations, particularly Traditionalists, prefer to receive phone calls, especially for business. For them, texting is what you do with your kids, friends, and grandkids. We hear from the older generation that in order to communicate with their children, they have to use the child's preferred way because it's the only way they will hear from them, and it doesn't seem to matter how old that child is, fifteen or fifty! Correspondingly, the grandchild's perception of a grandparent is that they are "old-fashioned" if the only way to communicate with them is via a phone call. They see this as a major inconvenience.

Contrast this with the younger generations, particularly Millennials and Gen Zs. They want texts.

They don't want to call. For them, a phone call is the last resort. When Gen Z says they were "talking" to their friends, they likely never spoke a word; the communication was via text. The younger the generation, the more comfortable they are with texting as their primary form of communication. Most of the older generations don't share that appreciation for texting. Many will use it socially for asking if someone has time for a call, visit, or setting up a get-together or, again, to communicate with their kids/grandkids. But after one or two text responses, they want to go on to more traditional means of communicating—a call or a visit. These generational differences are important to note at home and at work.

Older generations are getting savvier, though. According to Pew Research, there has been significant technology adaptation by older generations (Baby Boomers and Traditionalists) in the past decade, including use of smartphones and engagement in social media. While the numbers still lag between the older generations and Gen X, Millennials, and Gen Z, the gap is closing.

We can probably find a silver lining from COVID-19 in that adapting to a safe lifestyle while the virus raged really forced a change since visiting with grandchildren was not recommended by the CDC for people over sixty-five. This motivated seniors to seek connection via FaceTime and keep track of the family via Instagram and other technologies they likely didn't use in the past.

Workplace issues arise when you are trying to "impose" your preferred method of communication on someone else without checking first. Consider again that young Realtor. If he sent information via text to his older clients, they may not have received them, particularly if they haven't adopted smartphone technology. If the older clients feel forced to communicate in ways they are not comfortable, they likely will find someone who will work with them on their terms.

Let's consider meetings as a part of this topic.

Younger generations are reliant on their devices. When meetings are called, they will often arrive with laptops, tablets, or smartphones and engage with them while "listening in" to the meeting. While they think they are being productive this way, this level of distraction can easily take a ten-minute meeting and drag it into an hour. Think of the meeting host who has called a meeting for team input for a decision. When devices are present and participants are engaged in email or other work, getting their buy-in or feedback often involves breaking their attention away from the device and filling them in on what the rest of the group has been discussing in order to get agreement. This is a tremendous waste of time for the group, not to mention very disrespectful of the group's time. This gets worse with Zoom meetings, where the camera can be on and the person looks like they're engaged, or the camera is off. A lot of distractions occur that cause people to tune out important discussions.

In these cases, I encourage the meeting host to call a short meeting, set the ground rules that require full attention (i.e., no devices if in person), and then keep it short. If ten-minute tech-free meetings can grow to be the norm, people will leave their devices. But then it is incumbent on the host to have a set agenda and timeline and keep that meeting short!

Generational Intelligence Tools Applied to Cultural Intelligence

In the memorandum of understanding for a Rotary Grant I ran with a sister club in Indonesia, the Indonesian club was required to send me monthly financial updates. What I first received was not anything I was comfortable with—handwritten or computer-generated lists of expenditures, documents with stamps that served as receipts for monies expended. In short, this type of financial documentation was not what I had expected or felt confident with.

So I got on a plane and got an education. I learned that the electronic banking standards that I take as the norm are not the practice where our grant was being managed. This was the land of handwritten entries in bank passbooks, and most transactions were conducted in cash in fifty thousand or larger Rupiah notes. At the time, a fifty thousand Rupiah note was equivalent to approximately five dollars. It reset my expectations for the project's financial transactions. A blind man in a remote village providing handwoven bamboo twine for the project would be paid in cash with a handwritten receipt scribbled on a scrap of paper. Requiring documentation using current US technologies was not realistic, and I realized that my bias needed to be put in check, and I adapted to their method for documenting the transactions.

The experience of being there and seeing these transactions formed my expectations going forward. Using the skills associated with generational intelligence allowed me to reset my expectations due to cultural differences. As I said, it was an education, and it changed my worldview.

Communicating via Email

I prefer email to all other forms of communication for business because a written record of commitments and expectations is kept. When things are written down, there is much less room for the "Well, I remember it differently" discussion. But sometimes complex issues need a meeting or a phone call and require documentation after the fact. Further, I have learned the hard way that staff do not always read emails, or they may read them but not respond.

One thing I have learned about younger generations and email: no response *is* a response. If I am expecting a tangible response back, I make sure to make that clear *up front*.

Running a small start-up business, I've accepted the need to work weekends, usually doing the admin, personnel, and financial tasks. Once COVID-19 hit, I also started doing a lot of work that either needed to be shared with the team or needed responses back from the team, which I would do via email. I had one Millennial employee who would get angry on Monday morning when they would see five or ten emails generated over the weekend by me. They didn't like having to get caught up on Monday morning or feel at the start of the work week that they were already running behind. So to keep the peace, I limited my output to that individual on weekends and queued up what was needed for arrival late morning on Monday.

Ask yourself: Are you willing to compromise? When it comes to addressing communication challenges in the workforce, it's important to compromise for the sake of the team. In doing so, you must first recognize what your own preferences are, and then get in the habit of asking others about their preferences.

* * *

Generational intelligence means being aware of others' experiences or worldviews, understanding their preferences, and using this information to adapt and better collaborate. Once you're aware of others' different expectations and preferences, it's easier to reset your own expectations when needed.

Author, educator, and cultural anthropologist Angeles Arrien once said, "Four rules for life: Show up. Pay attention. Tell the truth. Don't be attached to the results."

A psychologist I know would often quote Arrien and observe that most people will naturally do three of four of these rules but be challenged by one. To stay on top of communication challenges, Arrien's rule of "pay attention" governs all.

The skills associated with generational intelligence—including awareness and curiosity of worldviews, recognizing personal biases and how that impacts your assumptions and expectations, and having a willingness to compromise—are important tools to finding the common ground to build relationships.

The bottom line: Communication challenges associated with generational intelligence can be remedied through awareness. Who wouldn't want the opportunity to make their organization better internally and improve their client relationships as well? The question "How do you want to receive your information?" needs to be asked. Begin asking today: How do you prefer to collaborate? Listen and leverage that information accordingly.

Go In:

In this reflective exercise, I invite you to get introspective as you consider this chapter's biggest takeaways.

- What are your own communication preferences?

- Have you observed or experienced a breakdown in communication due to generational preferences? How might you broker an arrangement with a coworker or client you need to exchange information with to benefit both of you?

- Can you think of a time when you became aware of an assumption you made about someone else's worldview that was wrong? How did you deal with it? Has someone made assumptions about you that were not correct? How did you correct their understanding?

CHAPTER TWO

Understanding Generational Motivators

We heard a story from a law firm. They wanted their youngest associates to bill a certain number of additional hours and were willing to pay them a substantial bonus if they hit the target. The senior attorneys were amazed by the large percentage of associates who did not make the goal, commenting that these Millennials were all lazy.

In fact, that was not the case at all. They were *not* lazy. The senior staff had used a form of motivation that had worked for themselves back in the day and had not taken the time to consider what would motivate this young crop of attorneys. As it turned out, the younger attorneys were motivated to do the additional work when the reward was additional time off at a quieter period.

How each generation's contributions are recognized may vary as well. If we generalize by generation, Traditionalists want to be respected or see that their experience is respected. Baby Boomers want to be valued. Gen Xers want to know they are bringing value to the table. Millennials want to know their personal impact on an outcome. However, how to recognize the *individual* is what the employer needs to know to keep that person engaged and contributing, and that takes time and energy to find out.

Motivation is personal.

Everyone has their own reasons for stepping up to a challenge, or not. I've struggled with this throughout my three decades in management and advisory positions. Personally, I have an overdeveloped drive to perform. It doesn't matter the task; I always seek to do the best I can. This causes me issues when I meet someone who is happy with doing the minimum needed to get by, or worse, either doesn't want to do the job or can't do the job and avoids being honest about it. So when we talk about how to get people to work beyond their current productivity level, the first thing to discern is whether motivation is the factor or if an ability or knowledge gap exists that is keeping the individual from performing as you expect.

If they have the knowledge and ability, then it is a motivational factor. Individuals who are seeking promotion and more responsibility are very easy to motivate. You need to make sure you have enough structure in your organization so they can make incremental steps up your organizational ladder.

If an individual is motivated by recognition, then you need to make sure your organization has the ability for incremental recognitions such as employee of the month, special parking spaces, small bonuses, and the like.

There are those, however, who are content doing what they do, and they are more challenging to motivate. If you need more out of them for a specific task or period of time, having a personal conversation and asking them to do this for you is probably the most effective tool. It's motivation from the perspective of being personally asked, of getting that one-on-one time with the boss, where their contribution is recognized and appreciated.

Then there are those who only want to do the job as they define it, as they feel they are obligated to do it. It's really tough to move their needle. These are the individuals who you want to make sure you see demonstrate the ability to perform a job for a sustained period of time before giving them the promotion and title. If you jump the gun with these folks with a title and responsibility, they will saddle you with their definition of acceptable, and it will be a long road to termination.

Recognizing Motivational Challenges

The first step in addressing workplace motivational challenges is to make sure everyone knows *what* they are working for, be it the success of a client, organizational sustainability, a new product launch, or other goal.

I look at motivation in terms of employment as the general desire or willingness of someone to do something, where the "something" is the task associated with their job. Sometimes they need to step up in a significant way and give more than the usual due to time constraints on a project: new work in, changing requirements, being short-staffed, or other reasons.

With strongly self-motivated people who understand what they are working toward and from where they draw a sense of purpose, there is a willingness to do whatever is needed for the job. In this case, it's important to monitor them to make sure they are not burning out or putting forth more than required, so you have that reserve to draw upon when you need it. (Note to CEOs: The same applies to you—you need to keep some in reserve for when you need to dig deep.)

This self-motivation is also called intrinsic motivation. Intrinsic motivation is characterized by an inner drive based on individual strengths and talents, like pride in a job well done.

Purpose-driven organizations seem to be gaining strength and popularity these days. These kinds of organizations are using purpose to create deeper connections with consumers, do more for the communities with which they work, and attract and retain talent and in the process are achieving greater results and impact. According to Deloitte, purpose-driven companies witness higher market share gains and grow three times faster on average than their com-

> **With strongly self-motivated people who understand what they are working toward and from where they draw a sense of purpose, there is a willingness to do whatever is needed for the job.**

petitors, all while achieving higher workforce and customer satisfaction.[6]

In contrast to this is extrinsic motivation. Extrinsic motivation is characterized by external sets of expectations, rewards, and punishments, like gold stars, participation trophies, and performance bonuses.

In addition to understanding motivations, you have to be reasonable in what you ask of your team. I like the analogy of a rubber band. We all have just so much elasticity. We can operate at a higher level for a while, like pulling a rubber band to its limit. But a rubber band only has so much give. When it gets pushed past its limit, it breaks. You want to know what that breaking point is and make sure you never ask for more than that, unless you are willing to lose key assets.

Years ago, I managed a team with what seemed to be an impossible task. I made sure we all knew what we were working toward, and to get there we did shift work and worked extremely long and uncompensated hours. But I made sure I knew what each person in

---

6   Diana O'Brien, Andy Main, Suzanne Kounkel, and Anthony R. Stephan, "Purpose Is Everything," Deloitte, October 15, 2019, https://www2.deloitte.com/us/en/insights/topics/marketing-and-sales-operations/global-marketing-trends/2020/purpose-driven-companies.html.

the team was working for, and I saw that my job as their manager was to seek a reward along their professional paths commensurate to the effort they gave the project. One wanted a promotion, one wanted a transfer to a different division, one wanted recognition, a couple wanted good raises, and a few were motivated by bonus checks. To their credit, they did what they needed to do to get us to success. And I, as their manager and the one who had asked them to step up for the better part of a year, forgoing vacations, made sure every one of them saw the reward they were working for. It was interesting that my manager did not do the same for me, so after completing this very intense work period, where I was performing a job well above what I was titled for, I walked into a senior executive's office, made my case, and was promoted on the spot. But that's another story, and one that has strongly shaped my vision of recognition to this day.

Setting motivations and rewards, at its fundamental level, is about relationship building, knowing what motivates the individual, understanding individual limitations, and ensuring your organization has the options necessary to be able to reward those individuals for exceptional performance.

One thing I believe: Organizations must be ruthless when it comes to rejecting individuals who aren't a great fit. Even if they come across as a high performer, they can wreak havoc on a positive, collaborative culture if they don't fit. They can be a demotivating force.

Addressing Generational Motivations

Traditionalists are motivated by money and respect. Motivators for Baby Boomers are money, nonmonetary rewards, and recognition. Gen Xers like monetary and nonmonetary rewards and place a high value on feedback. Millennials are motivated by moving up in an organization, professional development, and feedback. Generation Zs are motivated more by social than financial rewards, and their successes will be immediately shared on social media.

One motivation that is often neglected is gratitude, and this goes across all generations. Evidence suggests that gratitude and appreciation contribute to the kinds of workplace environments where employees actually want to come to work. It can be a motivating force. But be careful not to confuse gratitude with recognition.

Consider individual and generational aspects when you look to express appreciation. Someone who understands the power of gratitude will tend to be a much stronger motivator. If I ask my employees to do something out of the norm, I explain why it's important and they'll step up, understanding the need and that I'd be appreciative of it. If you want your team to go the extra mile, you need to ask for it and then show your gratitude. Gratitude needs to be factored into your way of doing business, even if it makes you uncomfortable.

Gratitude needs to be factored into your way of doing business, even if it makes you uncomfortable.

In our cohorts, we do an exercise with dollar bills. We start by ripping up dollar bills. Tearing money in half really gets people's attention. We then pair up participants, give them each a dollar half, and challenge them to get the other half from their partner.

We see three major categories of resolution to this challenge. There are those who see it as a win/lose challenge and will do anything to win. Others take a collaborative approach and plan to get a cup of coffee together and use the dollar to achieve that goal. Then there are the givers who are motivated by letting the other person have their half because they have the greater need.

Some of the motivators experienced in this exercise are: money, achievement, status (winning), power, autonomy (having personal control), mastery (getting better at something), and purpose (something greater than oneself). While I would like to say that there are clear generational trends in this, there aren't. The trends are more gender related, with males being more competitive and females being more collaborative. Interestingly, the givers don't have a gender trend. It's an eye-opening exercise to help understand what motivates individuals.

* * *

It's important to get to know what generational motivators exist in your own workforce, reset your expectations, and understand that certain groups of people may not simply be "lazy"—they may just not be motivated.

The bottom line: using generational intelligence, you can discover what motivates not only yourself but also the people you collaborate with and/or lead, so you might adjust your expectations accordingly. Be willing to step up and do things that may be out of your comfort zone or inconvenient—this includes simply paying attention, being willing to work with different personalities, understanding others' worldviews, and expressing your gratitude. There are rewards for all.

Go In:

In this reflective exercise, I invite you to get introspective as you consider this chapter's biggest takeaways.

- Rank these motivators as each applies to you: money, achievement, status, power, autonomy, mastery, purpose, gratitude, and social recognition.

- Using generational intelligence, how would you determine what would motivate an age-other coworker?

- Can you think of a time when you assumed that a coworker would appreciate a certain reward that, on second thought, possibly didn't align with their generational category?

CHAPTER THREE

Understanding How Teams Work

About thirty years ago, I started a new job with a new company. I found that the job was not so much about being an engineer, although those skills were needed for the job. It was more about getting people to work collaboratively.

My first task was getting nine separate organizations to agree to a set of requirements for a simulation capability that would be used in many systems, saving hundreds of millions of dollars in the life-cycle costs. That did happen, but the path to success was like blazing a new trail in the mountains in search of the highest peak when you don't have a map. Just when you get to the local peak, you realize there is another, higher one. You pick a path from many choices, and sometimes it works, sometimes it doesn't, and sometimes it takes you to an entirely different mountain range.

I was lucky and able to see this common system approach through to implementation and sustainment. It's still going strong, and others have adopted our model. But the first task was not easy. Each of the individuals involved had their own opinions, egos, motivations, and reasons for either being cooperative or stonewalling the project.

Back then, the generational differences were blurred a bit because almost all of us had been raised in an authoritarian environment. Surviving and being effective in that environment was tricky because people had defined their turf, and they wanted to do things their way. But for this approach to succeed, they had to adopt a complete paradigm change.

> **Every generation in the workforce today has experienced change and will face more. It is one thing that we all have in common.**

Change is hard, and it doesn't matter how old you are. Every generation in the workforce today has experienced change and will face more. It is one thing that we all have in common.

We are given *opportunity* for change, opportunities to adapt. All of these changes have and will continue to form generational differences—from technological to ideological ones—that should be kept in mind when collaborating as a team. The individuals who were asked to adopt a new paradigm eventually saw the value proposition. Time has shown that the progressive thinking adopted by these brave individuals has benefited everyone, including the bottom line. But adaptation was hard. Very different mindsets had to work together.

Recognizing Team Challenges

While at IBM, I was selected to attend their shortened IBM sales school for Federal Systems hard chargers. Initially touted as a boondoggle, a week out of the plant to play, it turned into the most competitive and formative week of my life.

Each day started with a sales rally full of hype, loud music, singing "our song," and getting worked up by the trainers. This was followed by an information session, and then it was into the trenches with our advisors who put us through role-play after role-play. From the time we arrived, the evening before day one, and through the first day, we were encouraged to relax, have fun, and get to know people. I took that at face value, not having had anyone to coach me in what was about to come.

The second day everything changed. At the sales rally, they gave special recognitions to a small handful of participants who distinguished themselves the first day. "Keys" were handed out—four-by-eight-inch printed pieces of paper with the image of a skeleton key on it. Each mentor could select one from their group of fifteen to recognize with a key. We all did the math that morning and realized that we only had three more chances at a key. From that point on, everyone was your competition for getting a key. The key I earned is something I have cherished in the three decades since. Most went home without a key.

This week was a life-changing experience for me. In addition to IBM's planned sales call methodology, I learned "objection handling." Objection handling is another form of *active listening*. It's engaging in a discussion to understand the "why" behind the objection, which is often something that can be resolved.

In the position that required me to build collaboration across the many different organizations, I used my objection-handling skills extensively. Within three months, I had gained the support of everyone. This was seen as a significant milestone for success in developing the common system. It was also at that point I realized that simple communications skills were often not practiced in business; otherwise, the coming together of this group would have happened a year earlier and would not have been seen as such a huge accomplishment on my part.

Where things get confused is when the goal or problem being solved is not well defined or the scope keeps changing. An epic example of this is the development of the Bradley Fighting Vehicle, memorialized in the hilarious movie *The Pentagon Wars*. Almost two decades and billions of dollars were spent developing a warfighter capability that was continually changed as stakeholders changed. It is a great example of how *not* to develop a product.

It is also worth noting that, at this point in time, the Traditionalists were in charge. These individuals lead with authoritarian leadership styles. It was a tough environment for collaboration. Most programs were run by edict. It was further validation to me of the value of objection handling/active listening.

It seems today that everything happens through collaborative work. It's difficult for *one* person to have all the knowledge required to take on even moderate-sized tasking. From an engineering sense, you need to involve program managers, finance folks, systems engineers, software engineers, test engineers—and that's just to start. From a business perspective, the launch of a new product then involves sales and marketing, which drives website updates, advertising, social media campaigns, and so forth.

Through it all team members must navigate generational differences in team engagement in order to find success.

Addressing Generational Differences in Team Engagement

Teamwork is the norm today. But the past experiences of individual members can bring biases and expectations into how teams should work together, which can cause problems.

Through it all team members must navigate generational differences in team engagement in order to find success.

Generational differences play into team dynamics in an interesting way. Let's consider tasking and collaboration. Younger generations want to be given a task with the freedom to figure it out on their own. They leverage a number of resources, like YouTube videos, to gain their knowledge. Older generations sought knowledge from peers or superiors since, in their day, the access to and availability of information was more restrictive. Not so today with the internet, explainer videos, and crowdsourced intelligence.

Let's consider teamwork experience. Millennials have been working in teams since elementary school. Their team experiences in school were primarily with others of the same age and/or experience level. Boomers and Traditionalists had more independent learning experiences; doing work as a team was not the norm in their education. This experience for older generations set expectations for deference due to seniority, experience, and knowledge. They worked hard for their senior position and the perks that came with them. They may be waiting to be consulted, which may not work with the younger generational paradigm of working independently to figure things out on their own. If these groups are not talking about their differing expectations for how the team will operate, and coming to a collective agreement, there will likely be issues.

For an organization, the mindset of younger generations to go off and learn themselves comes with risks and rewards. The tangible risk is that there will be a loss of the lessons learned from senior staff, resulting in avoidable mistakes, and loss of mentoring opportunities. On the benefit side, sometimes a fresh look can bring innovation into an organization, its products, and processes.

Another risk is that the younger generation, when stuck, may not seek help in a timely fashion. They may continue to flail and fail on their tasking.

A common ground needs to be found with the individuals working together—and this happens through communication.

Effective teams need a number of things, but the most important is the ability for individuals to express ideas without fear. It takes strong soft skills to create and maintain that culture. And it occurs best when it is organization-wide and not just central to the team.

> **Effective teams need a number of things, but the most important is the ability for individuals to express ideas without fear.**

You can think of most transactions as "teamwork." Just like a team launching a new product is working to solve a defined problem, a salesperson is working with a client to solve that client's issue, be it the need for a car, a new home, a replacement dishwasher, life insurance, and so forth. A team can be made up from as few as two people with the common interest or direction to solve a specific problem or achieve a specific goal.

One of the reasons many new committees start with developing their mission or charter is to ensure the participants are on the same page. Every time a team is brought together, they collectively need to define what their goals are and build out their tasks and schedule from that point. A team that does not have a common and appropriate goal cannot succeed except by chance.

> **A team that does not have a common and appropriate goal cannot succeed except by chance.**

Getting people to work better together means looking at the project at hand as a whole—and it's the same sort of thing when you're having generational challenges.

For example, if I was working one-on-one with someone who disparaged Millennials and the way they work, complaining that the Millennial work ethic was not up to par, I'd pull the thread on it and become an active listener. We'd identify the specific issue with the individual and get rid of the stereotype bashing. That's when the response gets slower. Maybe valid gripes are there, but they can then be addressed, and we can begin to consider looking at things differently, pointing out how these issues can be viewed from a different perspective—a generational perspective. Using generational intelligence, we'd learn what this Millennial may have had to deal with and what their motivations might be, and then we'd adjust how we deal with the issue going forward. Maybe that means a Boomer or Traditionalist has to adapt the way they work for the benefit of the group. By listening and being open to learning these things about yourself and your coworkers, you can change your entire work environment for the better.

One word of caution to leadership: be on the alert for individuals who like to be heroes. These are the folks who have a great idea that will guide the team initially in a specific direction but then won't support the team until they are on the verge of failing. At that point, they swoop in, solve all the problems, and bask in their self-created glory. These individuals are very disruptive to morale and to the health of an organization. They are best used in solitary environments where they can be their own heroes. They are difficult to spot initially, but if you pay attention to the pattern of team progress and dynamics, you will be able to spot these disruptors.

* * *

Building a better team that works more effectively together requires a different set of collaboration skills—skills fueled by generational intelligence. Many teamwork problems are generational issues due to differences in expectations and communication styles.

The bottom line: The generational differences in how individuals were raised, resulting in their different worldviews, can significantly impact how a team works if expectations of the individuals are not addressed and if the purpose of the team's work is not well defined. So factor in the time to have these discussions. Set clear goals and progress points for your teams. And make sure all members have ownership of those goals.

Go In:

In this reflective exercise, I invite you to get introspective as you consider this chapter's biggest takeaways.

- How do you prefer to work, alone or collaboratively?

- Whom do you have a hard time collaborating with? Get introspective and identify those issues so you can address them.

- Ask your team members what issues they're having. Practice active listening when they answer you.

Overcoming Biases

I've had great successes and a few challenges hiring Gen Z staff. One story involves a young woman who worked for us for a few months as an intern. She did not report to me directly, but I know that we were happy with her products and her production rate. However, toward the end of that period, she stopped showing up. She told us she was busy at school and wanted us to let her work remotely and independently. At that point in time, we were working very collaboratively, and remote work neither fit with our work process, nor was it appropriate with an intern at her level of experience. In response to her request, we told her she was expected in the office to work with the team. She did not come in or communicate with her supervisor for a week, after which we called to terminate her. It was a shock to her that we would do that. She didn't comprehend the importance of working with the group. She wanted to be independent and assumed that was her prerogative. She assumed that because we had been very happy with her prior work, it would give her license to conduct herself as she saw fit, even if it did not fit within the specifics of her work agreement. I also believe that she wanted to avoid a conflict and so chose not to tell us she would not be in. She just didn't show.

That was a shame. But just because we had concerns with this Gen Z doesn't mean this has been the case across the board.

I have three Gen Zs on my team today who are awesome people and engaging, independent workers. They're reliable and able to complete a task. Two of the three work together. The other works independently. Because of COVID-19 and the impact it had on our business, all three of them now work directly for me and are remotely working.

I attribute a few things to their happiness. First, I am willing to spend money on computers and software. These individuals have grown up with technology. The last thing I want to do is frustrate them from a tool or equipment perspective. Second, while I am specific about their tasking, I give them the resources, responsibility, and authority to get it done. As Gen Zs, they want some autonomy in their work. They know they have to complete what has been requested, but they have freedom in how they get it done. And they have freedom to choose their own schedules as long as they meet the deadlines and are available for our weekly meet-ups, which I am flexible in scheduling should their needs change. Third, I keep them involved in the big picture side of things, and I meet with them for fifteen to thirty minutes every week to learn what they are working on, what their front load is, and what their head-hurters are and allow them to ask me anything. Fourth, I look at these individuals as the entrepreneurs of tomorrow, so I share with them aspects of my job that they would not otherwise have access to. I am transparent with them on our successes and our failures. Fifth, I ask them for their insights. These individuals are incredibly insightful, and I have learned to listen to them. Lastly, I tell them how they are valued. Recognition is important. Gratitude is important. In my day, the next promotion is what we worked for. Today, it's more than that. They want a sense of ownership. They want to see how they are contributing to the success of the organization. They want to learn and grow in their jobs. And they want to be recognized financially.

I wish I had been able to work directly with and try to change the outcome of the first Gen Z

I mentioned. But what she wanted long term as an individual may have differed from what we could offer at that time. Luckily, regularly employing generational intelligence has allowed my team and me to become better at recognizing our own biases, and we are quick to consider the individual first while also keeping in mind how that person's generational experience should impact our reactions. It's great that many Gen Zs want to feel valued, offer their own creative insights, and be a part of the solutions—why wouldn't we want to incorporate their vision and that of every generation in today's workforce into our culture?

Recognizing Biases

One of the things I have seen in my decades of working as an employee, then as consultant, and now running my own business is that bias and stereotyping are heavily present in the workforce and usually *don't* bear out if you take a deeper look.

I grew up and went into "hard science" at a time when it was very unusual for a woman to follow that path. I managed a successful career, was a dedicated and hard worker, and I raised two children as a single mother. I did have help. But I ignored the stereotypes that defined women of the 1970s and 1980s, I fought past the biases that created traditional barriers by working harder and smarter than those around me, and I blazed my own path. And many successful individuals will tell you the same thing.

When my children were young, I accepted a part-time job with a major corporation. The terms of employment were that I worked four full days a week with Thursdays off. This was what I had requested, and they had agreed to it. But they wanted me on their management team, which by corporate edict required a standard full-time position. To get me to give up my one day off, they would schedule all critical meetings on my day off to demonstrate that I could work full time since they knew my work ethic meant I would be there for the meetings. They then pressured me to go full time and step into management. While I did not want the job, I was surprised at the rigidity of thought that only full-time people could manage. I wound up feeling disrespected and eventually resigned. That bias regarding full-time work to be a manager was eventually overturned when one of their rising stars, a woman in management who was expecting twins, decided to return to work part time postpartum. They allowed her to keep her position rather than losing her too.

Our culture has stereotypes for most things. There are stereotypes for genders, country of origin, career categories, and even dogs. Who hasn't heard that pit bull dogs are dangerous, when most owners of pits will describe them as sweet dogs? Of course, dogs that have not been appropriately socialized will be dangerous, but that is true for any dog, not just pits.

The bottom line is that stereotypes are just another form of prejudice. Our challenge is to know when we are biased and to take the time to know *the individual* rather than casting judgments from what we see and assume.

> **Our challenge is to know when we are biased and to take the time to know *the individual* rather than casting judgments from what we see and assume.**

From birth on, we are heavily influenced by our parents, our peers, and the media, and this is what establishes our biases at an early age. The good news is that with awareness, those biases can be overturned.

Traditionalists are stereotyped as "authoritarians," having a dictatorial leadership style. They are stereotyped as wanting to follow the rules. They may see younger generations as too willing to share personal information.

Contrast that to a Millennial who came of age with smartphone and internet technology, or the Gen Z who has had this tech at their fingertips for most of their lives. These experiences impact how an individual responds to stimuli. A Traditionalist might be comfortable with being patient while an older computer boots up because they can vividly remember the time before computers, and they see this device as still meeting their needs. Meanwhile, a Millennial may expect a computer to respond almost instantaneously and gets impatient when that doesn't happen. The Traditionalist may view that Millennial as being "entitled" or "impatient." But the reality is that the Traditionalist is comfortable with being patient due to external factors that the Traditionalist grew up with. The Millennial did not have that same experience. Recall again that the Traditionalist grew up with a rotary phone and no way to leave a message if the number he was dialing was busy or unanswered. The Millennial has grown up being able to directly reach whomever they need to.

These technology differences have imparted significant differences in individual expectations. The reach and availability of mobile phone technology today are things that were beyond imaginable to the Traditionalist or Baby Boomer in their formative years. Add to that replacing slide rules with powerful home computers, replacing written correspondence with email and texting, and the incredible reach of the internet. We can understand how technology would strongly define personal behaviors like patience level as a generational characteristic. This is also why an individual's worldview can give rise to stereotyping as one generation views the behaviors of another.

A Traditionalist may have worked for one organization for their entire career while a Millennial may have job-hopped to satisfy their desire for continuous training, advancement, and salary growth. Each generation has experienced events that color their expectations from employers and what they want long term from an employer. The Great Recession of 2008 impacted a young generation that saw parents lose their jobs. Their stability factor lies within themselves as a result, and you may not see them having loyalty to an organization. Does that mean you should avoid hiring Gen Zs as a result? Absolutely not. But you should be aware of the influences on the generation's worldview, and then address it with the *individual*.

Addressing Bias through Generational Intelligence

We all have biases, but the danger lies in when we don't recognize that we have biases. To address bias one needs to know their own biases, and rather than making assumptions based on those biases, one needs to get to know the individual. Using generational intelligence skills can often give you the insights to interpret actions and outcomes.

> We all have biases, but the danger lies in when we don't recognize that we have biases.

A Millennial may seem impatient and entitled to a Traditionalist, but that Traditionalist grew up in an environment where researching a topic took significant effort, including trips to the library, reliance on a good librarian to get that right article, waiting while an article was copied and mailed from another source, and so on. A Millennial or Gen Z has all of that and more on their phone, immediately. They are used to crowdsourcing for information and resources, something a Traditionalist might not be comfortable with, understand, or be aware of. These are generational differences. Understanding those differences is helpful to understand the "why" behind behaviors. However, they should not be used predictively.

I once consulted with a manufacturer that had a problem with younger generations showing up on time. When you have an assembly line going and one guy is late to work, the organization's productivity is impacted. That is a serious problem. The manager reported that this individual felt that they should have the flexibility to arrive and finish up when they want. Clearly, either that employee needed to be educated in the "why" of showing up on time (to maintain the production schedule), and if that was not sufficient to motivate them, then they should not be working for an organization in a job that requires them to adhere to rigid time requirements. This is about alignment of personal brand with organizational culture and, if not done up front, can get very expensive for the hiring organization. While I don't run assembly lines, I listen to people who do, and this is a common issue that they're seeing from the younger generations.

There are patterns that are attributed to each of the generations in the workforce. These are insightful to understanding the "why" behind an individual's behaviors but should not be used for prediction or judgment on the part of an individual.

* * *

The insights imparted in this book are meant to challenge you to recognize and address multigenerational workplace issues. This will lead to better communications and better team dynamics, which should ultimately improve productivity and benefit your organization's bottom line while creating a better work environment for your staff.

Each generation has experienced things that contribute to that generation's worldview. These worldviews color an individual's expectations of their employment, motivational factors, and workplace needs.

The bottom line: Awareness of the generational experiences that shape individuals is one more way we can use generational intelligence to address coworker conflicts, learn what each employee's motivators are, and become better communicators, better colleagues, and better teams. Additionally, generational intelligence should be added as an integral part of professional development training in every organization.

Go In:

In this reflective exercise, I invite you to get introspective as you consider this chapter's biggest takeaways.

- What are some preconceived biases you have on one of the five generations that currently make up the workforce?

- Can you think of an issue you have with an age-other colleague? How can you use generational intelligence to address that issue with him or her as an individual?

- What events in your lifetime do you think have informed your own set of biases?

CONCLUSION

I f your workplace participated in the phone exercise I mentioned in this book's introduction, how would you have done? Do you think you'd have preset expectations about where everyone would stand? Do you think you could be surprised by which phone best represents a colleague's experience? What have you learned over the course of these chapters about your own biases, motivations, and preferences for communicating and collaborating?

As we close, I hope you can see how every chapter's themes—communication, motivations, teamwork, and biases—coalesce when it comes to understanding and solving workplace challenges using generational intelligence. This other soft skill is our window into addressing multigenerational challenges since the impacts of not understanding people are significant.

Exploring how to improve workplace situations through generational intelligence can only help productivity. Understanding how life experiences have shaped all five generations in today's workforce—Traditionalist, Baby Boomer, Gen X, Millennial, and Gen Z—can alter our biases, adjust our expectations, and help us be better communicators, collaborators, and team members. Knowing what motivates age-other individuals and differing personalities requires active listening skills and relentless awareness, including self-awareness. Remember, there are rewards for all, and they are not all the same.

This other soft skill is our window into addressing multigenerational challenges since the impacts of not understanding people are significant.

Be patient. Remember, developing strong soft skills, especially the other soft skill—generational intelligence—takes awareness, time, and energy. Everyone deserves to feel valued and happy and to thrive at work. A generationally intelligent organization will provide an environment to foster a positive culture and professional growth, which will benefit the organization as well.

ACKNOWLEDGMENTS

This book was written from a lifetime of experience and the many people with whom I gained that experience.

Starting chronologically, I must recognize my parents and the advantages they provided me, from education to the way I was reared. My dad pushed me to be the best of my abilities. My mom strove to teach me to listen first, speak later. Those who know me will recognize that this is a skill I am still working to master.

I must thank every colleague, employee, advisor, mentor, boss, customer, client, and friend who gave me the opportunity to learn from challenging situations. These individuals are too numerous to name individually. You know who you are.

I am forever grateful to my daughters, Dana and Mary, for providing me with the best opportunities to learn how to be a mom and giving me firsthand experience into what it means to be a Millennial in a Boomer's household and vice versa.

The importance of Rotary International and my membership in the Rotary Club of Tarpon Springs cannot be overstated. This organization has given me a world of mentorship that has guided my outlook on volunteerism, opened doors, and provided me the advice I needed to launch my company, Alpha UMi. I've also learned that volunteers prefer to be asked— no one wants to be "volun-told."

I thank Jean Coleman and Robin Wikle. I will forever be in debt to these two creative dynamos. I also want to recognize Carl Treleaven, Charles Dean, and David Chitester, whose insights into the world of entrepreneurship have strongly built my vision for my company.

All experiences shared in this book are colored by my perspective and blurred by the passing of time. Thank you, kind reader, for understanding this.

ABOUT THE AUTHOR

Carrie Root, PhD (mechanical engineering), is the founder and CEO of Alpha UMi, Inc., an innovative company committed to authoring exceptional professional development training curricula for use in industry and academia. In 2020, Alpha UMi's curricula received certification by the National Council for Continuing Education and Training.

With over thirty years' experience in management, consulting, and advising, preceded by working for various companies as small as one hundred employees to *Fortune* 500 companies, Carrie has a proven track record for bringing innovative and strategic solutions to the organizations she serves. To learn more about Carrie, find her on LinkedIn at https://www.linkedin.com/in/carrie-root-phd-ultimate-troubleshooter/. To learn more about Alpha UMi and the products they offer, please visit http://www.5GPowerSkills.com.

GET IN TOUCH

Alpha UMi offers innovative training programs to elevate professionalism, grow leadership, and develop strong soft skills. Our training programs are transformative, engaging, affordable, and will make all the difference. To learn more, go to https://www.5GPowerSkills.com, or email us at info@5GPowerSkills.com.

Keep up with trends and what's happening by signing up for our monthly newsletter on our website, https://www.5GPowerSkills.com.

Dr. Carrie Root is available for workshops on generational intelligence and many other topics. Please contact her at Carrie.Root@AlphaUMiInc.com or via LinkedIn at https://www.linkedin.com/in/carrie-root-phd-ultimate-troubleshooter/.

OUR MOTIVATING
MUSIC PLAYLIST

A t Alpha UMi, we enjoy leveraging technology to share our ideas, our recommendations, and our favorite music. Sometimes it is just fun to know what other people listen to!

For this book, the Alpha UMi staff has compiled a playlist of their favorite motivational music. To enjoy our music choices, scan the QR code, click the link that comes up, sign up for a free Spotify account if you do not have one (and endure the occasional commercials if you don't want to pay for a premium subscription), and hit play. Then prepare to be motivated!

We would love to hear what *you* listen to when you need to rev up! Please send us your favorite motivational songs. Just send the title and performer of your go-to, get-moving music to info@alphaumiinc.com.

Enjoy listening.

Printed in the USA
CPSIA information can be obtained
at www.ICGtesting.com
JSHW012044140824
68134JS00033B/3246

9 781642 252989